CERASUS
Magazine

Issue # 1

ISBN: 9798732563870

Editors:
Ashley Sapp & John Wilks

Website: cerasusmagazine.com

Contact: cerasusmag@gmail.com

Publisher: Cerasus Poetry, London N22 6LY

CONTRIBUTORS

Gale Acuff

Ed Ahern

IR Belletti

Alan Cohen

Milton Ehrlich

Jim Ferguson

Allie Kerper

Paweł Markiewicz

Bruach Mhor

Zach Murphy

Simon Nagel

Nidhi Panandikar

Yash Seyedbagheri

Penny Sharman

Shiyang Su

John Wilks

The Trail

Out, walking on the sand. The beach is empty of humans,
the tide has left a long line of multi-coloured periwinkles,
the trail-with-a-tail (south/south/west) may be an otter's.
Here I could think of anything: Russian ballerinas romanced
by doomed Bolsheviks, the decline of the tricorn hat,
the price of tin. But somehow the trail, the periwinkle line,
imaginary spinning ballerinas, shot Bolsheviks, tin cans,
three cornered hats---try as I may---they all lead to you.

Bruach Mhor

The Hitching Post

A man rested against a post in the shade beneath the eaves. The day was hot and slow. He enjoyed the heat and the passing cars from the street. "I'll stay in this spot for a long time," he thought, "and think about how much I'm enjoying this moment."

Fat thunderheads rolled in, bringing summer rain. The man leaned against the post some more, happy to get wet but not as happy as he was in the heat. "It'll come around again," he thought. He liked the sweet smell of the rain hitting the dirt.

His clothes soaked through waiting for the rain to stop. It didn't for a very long time. When the sun returned, he was surrounded by puddles. Several motorcycles drove down the street. They were loud and didn't remind the man of distant waves like the cars did. "It will never be the same again," he thought.

Simon Nagel

Street Corner Jam

Hot summer dusk in the city,
stripped down clothes, open windows,
traffic stopped for cross-walkers
at the street corner of music Babel.
Songs punch each other for place,
car raps wrestle with window gospels,
ped pods channel rock and bachata,
classical whimpers in under sound.
The round ends with a green light
and the musics go to neutral corners.

Ed Ahern

After

You could call.
But haven't.
I could call. But don't.

We are balanced
in our weak excuses,
distant and equidistant.

Though close enough
to hear each other's silence
almost as breath.

Bruach Mhor

Low Water Springs

So we can walk, no splash,
to a one-heron island in the bay;
pick some Sea lettuce, plenty,

a food as the name suggests.
The delight is the Sea grass:
slumped as if raced through.

Sea horses love Sea grass,
Dad says, with a straight face,
and white horses must graze.

Bruach Mhor

BBQ

Someone left a barbecue by the dumpster weeks ago. It was covered with rust and spiderwebs. A man stared at it for a long time one afternoon. The barbecue gave him a lot to think about.

The man told all his coworkers about the abandoned barbecue. They politely listened and went on with their business. No one collected the barbecue by the time he returned from work. He counted the number of cars capable of hauling it away in his neighborhood. He was disappointed.

The barbecue remained beside the dumpster for a month, which upset the man every time he emptied his garbage can. He told himself he'd write the city. He called about renting a trailer to haul it away, but couldn't commit to a price. Someone has to take it, he thought. It's the way of things.

Tall weeds grew around the barbecue. The man gently pulled them and maintained the ground near its base so it would look more attractive to potential takers.

A season passed and the barbecue was gone. It left behind four deep holes in the ground where its feet had stood. The man followed the fading trail of dirt in the direction it was taken. He took the rest of the day off.

Simon Nagel

Beach Hut

Dunster Beach 1956--2014

I wish I had a beach hut painted white, blue or shocking pink.
That's where time stands still, where she waits on the veranda
and gathers all the tiny paddlers in behind one door.

I remember being lost in the rolling pebbles, wet sand castles
and melting ice-creams. I remember the wild child, the screams
in the waves, the fantasy figurehead telling me I was in control.

Today the beach has slipped nearer to the sea and time has
stretched herself over the huts on Dunster beach. With closed eyes
my feet still run towards a fixed line on the horizon.

Penny Sharman

Aristocratic Diction

As if I were a peasant
Had never been to school
Spent all my days plowing, milking, restoring fences
And they, going by on horseback
Laughing, superior, looking down:
"Regardes; il travaille sans cesse"

As if, yes, eating my cabbage and turnips
In their soups and stews
They deem me, with exquisite justice, coarse and stupid
My words, like bricks, fixed hard and practical
Song out of my reach
Truth too complex for my toil-and-mud-disciplined mind

Alan Cohen

Gleaning The Attic

The purgatory of my possessions
reproaches me from the jumbled attic.
Dusty sleeping bags and thermal wear
cached for trips no longer taken.
Books on fishing and philosophy
long unnibbled except by paper lice.
An oversized, silver-plated tea service,
a present from a long-gone aunt,
blackened from never once being used.
Phonograph records from a dead mother
not played in several decades.
A concretion of things once treasured,
lacking any present grace or purpose,
hoping to be redeemed by new owners.

Ed Ahern

Rose Knows

Every autumn day Rose
passes by the hot air balloon field in
Stillwater, wishing she had enough money in
order to go up for just one ride.

Last winter had not just taken a toll on Rose, it took nearly everything
she had left. Now, she has a frostbitten toe and a frostbitten heart.

Rose knows that even the happiest golden leaves grow weary when they catch the
first gust of winter's harsh might. Rose knows that if the sun ever decides to go away
for good she'll try to make it promise to come back. Rose knows that if she would have
had her life together, her adopted boy Frankie would still talk to her.

Across the air balloon field, sits a pawn shop. A pawn shop is a depressing place when you've
got nothing to pawn, nothing to sell, and not enough means to buy anything. A job application
turns into a hopeless slate the moment you see "Three years of experience needed."

After staring at her weathered reflection in the pawn shop window, Rose turns around toward
the field and observes an unattended hot air balloon. She crosses through the dewy green
grass, looks around, and decides to hop into the balloon's gondola.

The balloon is much bigger than Rose thought it would be. Her eyes widen as she gazes
up at the balloon's bright rainbow colors. Suddenly, a pair of balloon tour guides run
toward her, yelling "Stop!"

Rose quickly unravels the ropes from the ground, boosts the propane
flame, and takes off into the sky. From this view, the falling leaves
look like fluttering butterflies. Rose knows that when she
comes down she'll be in a lot of trouble. So she squints
up at the sun and gives the balloon some more
power.

Zach Murphy

Between The Sand And The Stars

There are no easy ways
to not get blown away:
Take off your old pajamas
and take a Beretta shotgun
out from under your bed.
Climb up the tallest tree
and grab a bolt of lightning
in the next thunderstorm.
Use it to knock on the door
between heaven and earth.
Ask for a safe place to hide
before the stars disappear
in the heat of the sun's rays.
If life on earth is ending,
I don't want to be there when it happens.

Milton Ehrlich

My Favorite Day of The Week

... was always Saturday:
a weekly trip to Horn & Hardart for a lunch-
baked beans and Lemon Meringue pie-
and then a show at the Paramount
or Roxy, where Bobby-Soxers' idol,
Sinatra, sang,"I'll Never Smile Again,"
the swing of Harry James & Benny.
It was love at first sound
inspiring me to take up the trumpet
and start my own 12-piece band.
I saved every penny delivering newspapers
to buy an autogiro
like the one I saw at the'39 World's Fair,
since to get to those movie palaces
required a bus and subway,
and I couldn't wait to fly.

Milton Ehrlich

More Or Less

In mid-January, there's a break in the weather
and we go for a walk
and learn it's not just the camellias we see from the window.
Lithodora and rosemary both have new blue flowers;
there is, on heather and the odd azalea, a bleak but settled pink,
while the birch flaunts thousands of new catkins.
Most leaves are a bright green, bulbs are sprouting
and there are buds everywhere.
All this suggests that winter is our Dark Ages of the natural world;
most of which we miss, keeping indoors.
Not life and death then,
or growth and stasis,
but faster and slower,
larger and smaller,
hare and tortoise,
growth and growth.
More or less.

Alan Cohen

Terra Unfirma

One day I'm going to die   I don't want to but I've got no choice so so much for free will though of course there's free will and then there's free will   if I behave myself I can live forever   _eternally_ is how they put it down at Sunday School or maybe I should say _up there_   if I sin a lot less and do good deeds   a lot more of them   then when I'm dead and my soul goes to God to be judged then maybe I can squeak in   kind of like making the Hall of Fame on the last ballot of my last year of eligibility   man that was close   but either way   whether God gives me thumbs-up or –down   I'm going to speak what's on my mind at that time   what's left of it, my mind that is but then again my time as well   it will pretty much be up   there's no clock for eternity is what's ticking me   I'll tell God what's on my soul then   not that He won't know anyway but it will feel good just saying it forget I probably won't have lips, teeth, and tongue so maybe I'll just stand there   if I have legs   while God reads what's in my soul or heart or whatever   it would be easier all the way around if He would let folks just live forever on Earth I mean and not _as it is in Heaven_   ha ha   if He'd let us live forever on _terra firma_ and forget about perfection   Earth seems like the right place   it's good enough for me   like that old-time religion but when you die and go to Heaven you don't die at all   Heaven is just for God and Jesus and the Holy Ghost and angels and leave it to them while we go on and on on Earth and I think it's a pretty damn decent idea so after Sunday School this morning I hit Miss Hooker with it there on the plywood porch of our portable building   no one around   everyone gone home   just the two of us   man and woman even though I'm only 10   not a man yet but when that happens I'll think that it didn't take so long at all

and Miss Hooker my Sunday School teacher at 25   plenty
old enough to know better and even worse but anyway
then she sat on the top step and I warned her to beware
splinters   she wears her legs in stockings most of the time
at least when I see her   and pulled me down beside her and
said to me   I guess it was me she was talking to "Hon   if
nobody ever died then nobody could ever live"   which I can
only guess is from the Bible or one of those fancy-ass
calendars or a coffee table book   the kind with big pages
and lots of photos   even paintings and just a few choice
words here and there   or maybe the President said it and
probably not Ronald Reagan but then again probably so
Nancy   might've   helped   him   and   her   astrologer
helped <u>her</u> but anyway all I could say was "Y'know, I never
thought of that"   not that I knew what the Hell she was
talking about but then again that's President Reagan for
you so whatever she means it makes a lot of sense   it's
religion I guess   no one understands it but it packs the
churches on Sunday morning so then I told Miss Hooker
goodbye   I walk to church and back again and you can see
my house   well   my <u>parents'</u> house   they pay for it and I'm
just their only child   from here   the plywood porch that
Father helped build   not that he's been to church since   he
likes his sleep on weekends   and started for home and
about halfway across the parking lot I heard Miss Hooker
call   call my name so I turned around but she was gone
back inside our classroom I guess so if it wasn't she then it
had to be God or someone else in the Trinity or an angel or
a figmation of my imaginement   I called my <u>own</u> name
that is   and heard it but at the same time didn't and a
lifetime of this would kill me dead even if I lived forever

Gale Acuff

April Fools, 2014

On the last day the Beckside Bitches left the sanctuary of blackbird songs,
each carefully tying the laces of their walking boots.

In the moments before the dawn chorus a barn owl remembers them
and hoots to her mate in the art of the wood.

The weird sisters walk under the disused railway bridge, a portal
to the silences high on the ridge, the footpath to the Copper Mines.

The panorama is fit enough for a Wordsworth host, but the gold is
under the tread of boots, the wet mud of companionship.

The hum of a million bumbles, a common carder, a buff tail orchestra,
is a busyness of contentment.

The high banks talk of words and line breaks, of moss dynasties
and elfin towers, of rabbit fur and ancient rust in a tin bath.

Silently, in the final seconds, the pen nibs of hearts and hands are held
in the Lakeland and the Beckside Bitches turn heads and grin to the world.

Penny Sharman

The World Of The Living Dead

Everybody wants to know
what happens after you die.
I just got a report from a friend
who appeared in my dream.
He said not to worry — it's fun.
There's an open bar with celestial wine
to keep you drinking for all eternity.
When your spirit leaves your body
it's completely naked and travels
to a place that's much like Fire Island
where residents often run around naked
and no cars are allowed.
Like Plato's Retreat, free sex is encouraged
with a consenting partner — similar to policies
of the better nursing homes of today.
Forget about meeting up with loved ones.
There are just too many divine spirits floating around,
and there are no bulletin board notices with names
like in the post-holocaust period where relatives
tried to locate each other after being liberated
from concentration camps.
You're on your own like never before. Enjoy!

Milton Ehrlich

The Dreamery Inshore

(after *Shipwreck off a rocky coast* by Abraham Hulk The Elder)

A dreamed ship runs aground
in the most marvelous and dreamiest afterglow.
The mast adverts the orientation of
a tender Morning star.
Seafarers die at midnight
suffering the sea-froth fantasy.
The wind wrenches a canvas,
in search of a Golden Fleece,
towards piratical islands.
The sea sways
to the siren rhythm
of Terpsichorean art.
On the sandbank,
a letter in a bottle lies with
a sonnet to king Poseidon,
written by a dead sailor.
A rock inshore stands
as custodian of eternity,
waiting for Apollonian dreams.
A cloud emanates from
the meek paradise-heaven
and manifests the serious
weird of the moment.

Paweł Markiewicz

The Conversation

"How do you want to die?"

"Is that a threat?"

"I mean, like. . . If you could choose, which way would you prefer to die?"

"Thank God. I was worried for a second."

"And you can't say in your sleep. That's a copout. And a cliché."

"Aren't conversations about death a cliché?"

"Just answer the question."

"Hmm. . . Skydiving."

"Skydiving?"

"Think about it. You get that insane adrenaline rush as you're jumping out of the plane, and if something happens to go wrong, you'll hit the ground so fast that you probably won't even feel it."

"That sounds awful."

"You asked, and I answered. What would you pick?"

"I'd like to die up in space. It'd be so quiet and peaceful. Just floating out there surrounded by stars that have already experienced the same fate. . . Gazing at a magnificent view of the moon. . . It'd be the perfect way to go."

"That actually does sound pretty good."

“I have something to tell you.”

“Should I be sitting down?”

“You are sitting down.”

“Is it something that will freak me out?”

“I have terminal cancer.”

“What?”

“It’s on my spine. I just found out last week.”

“Fuck. Can’t the doctors do anything?”

“Nope. It wouldn’t do any good.”

“This only means one thing.”

“What’s that?”

“It means we have to start figuring out how to get up to space.”

Zach Murphy

The Unyielding Dead

Mass graves, I succumbed to and
only my mass failures left to write about.
Pieces of paper that scribble my anger,
crumpled away in their ash pits.

I am the fire they blow into,
the heat of the moment they flow into,
the beat of the drum they draw from
and I bleed simply to claw from.

I am dead to them and yet undead,
I am unyielding still,
an angry idea floating in their minds,
unharmed, until they stop and listen.

A revolution is coming and it's coming hard,
bullets of rubber are merely pieces of toys,
my spirit is harder than your weapons,
unnerving, for I'm stronger when you silence me.

Judge me not, by the color of my skin,
by shape of my bones,
you set this unprecedented precedence,
I now set an unyielding tone.

Nidhi Panandikar

My Sudden Loneliness On Saturday

It is Saturday evening and I suddenly feel
an ache around my waist:
a shining needle dances through
my bending spine and wakes
the whining of my broken body.
In the dying harmony,
my churning stomach
craves for a cheeseburger
and a bottle of Vienna beer;
my lonely thorax
needs a soft pillow to appease
the emptiness of a cold bed.
For my fatigued finger,
I expect to get
an aged stone, a polished
white-blue marble I once had at six;
the same, yet a bit larger.
I want it to have
& to hold tightly when it weeps.
Remind me for once and all,
I am not an oozing balloon under heaven
when I hear violet sun falling in dusk,
when I pass through orange streetlights
& feel the warmth of crowds and creamed pasta.
In chill wind,
I could still fasten my jacket and laugh
in a sentimental way,
not a miserable weeping,
like when I hold a marble in my hands:
firm and lasting,
an aged stone.

Shiyang Su

Rob The Boy, Kid

The white boy comes from southern Italy
and someone must have told him he was horrifying,
because that's what he tells me the day after he kissed me.

I swallow his words when he says he's saying it for me.
I don't believe him entirely from the start.

I giggle. The day before he was shaking.
He said it was because he was drunk,
but this can't be true.

The day of my first kiss
he interlocks his fingers with mine
and holds his chest and I get scared
and he tells me his heart is ill.
I believe him. He puts my palm on his sweaty shirt
and through it I feel more of his humanity
than he'll ever want to see of mine.

His kiss is dry.
He tells me to abuse him and I wonder what they did to him.
He tells me to stop feeling when I hug him and I wonder
who the hell took this boy and kicked him until he
became what he has become.

I laugh sadly and tell him this was my first kiss
and he looks at me like I am a cute two-year-old and I've just pissed myself.
Oh, no, he goes, *non ci credo.*

We sit together, afterwards.
My jumper is loose where he tugged at it
to make me stay.
I ruffled his hair and
this is the most intimate I'll ever be with someone
if I die within the next two years.

He throws rocks at the ants going for the break on the table
and tells me I'm a solid 2.
Our ugly friend is a 10 in his eyes, I wonder what they did to him
to make him so rude.
I break my own heart again because I don't even tell him
that he's not as beautiful as he thinks he is,
but maybe,
this is because nobody has ever messed with me
the way they messed with him.

He tells me that I don't have the courage to do anything
and to prove him wrong he tells me to kiss him.
I do.
I steal and take and rob him of all his lips can give me,
and then he tells me that he should have never kissed me.

He tells me he's in love with my friend who's another girl.

He tells me not to tell any of this to anybody, or
he will kill me.

IR Belletti

Excuses

It's easy to dredge up excuses. The world demands. Credit card payments, student loans, rent.

And it's especially easy to conjure illness, technological malfunctions, a dead sister.

Sometimes an excuse buys you a day. Sometimes two weeks.

It's better than cold truth.

At least you can tell yourself that people bought it. You are who you reveal yourself to be. And you've revealed someone who's just slipped for a moment, someone life's inflicted tragedy upon. Someone otherwise a paragon of responsibility.

Of course, you've been descending into a rabbit's hole for several years, light becoming fainter and fainter.

But you can't tell anyone that.

How do you talk of being a professor? And how do you talk department emails, rife with rules and norms? *Professionalism, dynamism, achievement, excellence, contribution.* The buzzwords strike you in cold Times New Roman. Walk this way, achieve this way, dress in Khakis and only the finest dress shirts.

You can expound about Richard Yates and suburban malaise in *Revolutionary Road.* Talk Hemingway's iceberg theory. You try to avoid failing students, even those who think *The Awakening* is an indie rock band. At least they're unabashed in their failure, replete with youthful cheer, even if mixed with hints of belligerence.
But you've never been nominated for an award.

How do you talk of emails celebrating colleagues and their myriad of publications? Each daily email proclaims Henry Chevalier's latest poetry collection or Janet DiCenzo's latest novel. They proclaim the prestige of the publisher, release dates and a few details about the inventiveness of said professor. *A novel in footnotes! A poetry collection in rap beats!*

You can't talk about your unborn book. About the inability to let words form among the footnotes and rap elegies. They're always telling you that some people are a little slower where achievement is concerned.

But that just makes nights before a computer ever the more excruciating, the electronic hum of screens arresting you. What could you come up with? Dysfunctional families in the suburbs? Cliché. Hopeful tales? Same.

On top of that, you get reminders from the department head, Dr. Edgar. Smile more, glad-hand students and colleagues.

"Don't be distant, old sport," he says.

You try to ask students about the shape and scope of their lives. They laugh or tell a joke. Occasionally, someone confides they got high or drunk. But they never speak of their goals, things they've achieved. Things they haven't.

You need a cheap drink after weeks and months of all that. Of course, one drink a week turns to five drinks a night. Five drinks turn to ten and maxed out cards. But the drinks are something all your own, your moment among the jukebox and the crash of balls at the pool table. A moment away from small apartments and cracked white walls.

You make no excuses for this. You have your own libations, a little booth, looking out onto streetlamps and swaths of night sky, something sorrowful, beautiful and vast. You even have your own community of drunks, people finding laughter when they stumble into the jukebox or spill a beer.

But then the cards keep maxing and you dip into the rent stash.

What else do you say? The media, even your own colleagues all talk of bootstraps. Ingenuity. Pulling yourself up. And they pronounce this with starched smiles, smiles with cracks. But no one comments on the cracks when you're smiling.

Don't talk about feelings. Every problem has a solution.

And what of credit card representatives, the landlord, everyone else?

Would they proclaim a modicum of sympathy? More likely, they'd retreat into awkwardness, find an excuse to retreat while you revealed things others learned to hide. They might proclaim some platitude. It's darkest before the dawn. Or they might offer a "sorry," something rushed and fleeting.

They might brush away the truth. Offer cold judgments. Tell you to enroll in this program or that program.

But the truth is, every company needs a reason for failure. Any reason. They insist on it. If you need help getting back on track, please call X. If you're having difficulty with rent payments, call Y. They want creativity.

So, you load up on the excuses while you try to pay off one card. Then another. Of course, you slip again on drinks. But you're down to two or three a night. That's progress.

And you pay half of one card off.

You should give up the excuses. And you will.

But at this juncture, you'd see a recovering, thirty-five year old professor. Gone would be the man who once despised whining. The youthful being who donned a sly smirk and told awkward historical jokes about the Romanovs and incest. Gone would be the man who once walked with a more graceful gait.

And the litany of what-ifs would rise to the top. *You could have chosen option X, you could have, you could have.*

Besides excuses are just a waystation. Something natural.

You reach out to the landlord. Establish payment plans. Draw up timelines.

Meanwhile, you dredge up more dead sisters, make yourself a hemophiliac, hemorrhaging weekly. You make up stories of fires and other destruction in your life.

Shame still rises with words sliding, but you bat it away.

It's a waystation. You'll beat the excuses.

Meanwhile, you get bombarded with more excuses on TV. They pepper courtroom dramas, sitcoms, debt relief commercials. *My ex-wife tried to castrate me, I forgot that the car was in drive, we can reduce your monthly payments if a train disfigured you.*

Your own students speak excuses too. Felled printers, broken clocks, even the occasional dog-ate-my homework tale.

Excuses keep contracting. They're contagious. Dead sisters turn into personal accidents and falls. An actual bootstrap is worked into another excuse.

You pay off a little more of a credit card. Maybe two-thirds now? You pay a month or two of rent too.

That's something.

But you won't make up more excuses. Soon. Very soon.

It's just a waystation.

Yash Seyedbagheri

Growing Up In An Italian Nowhere City

I am eleven years old and I want to leave my country.

I live in a village so small people joke
that my internet connection is shit.

I come from the place where things don't happen.

I write because daydreaming is the only way
to be sure I am still living the life
people tell me to live,
even if the sky is grey and the air is sticky
and my hair smells of the cheap perfumes
the stores use downtown.

I roam the center of the closest city until it becomes the map
of my own palm.

I hugged my crush for the first time here,
next to the corner behind the bank. It was
an ugly evening where the girls had all the same
black and red makeup
and we all complained that we would never be able to find a job.

I went to the high school there, behind the train station.
We organized ball nights and my girl friend I now know I had a crush on
kissed the other guy I had a crush on.
I see their tongues bright with alcohol and he's wearing a designer shirt,
but her dress was 20 euros.
I feel fat by the corner
and later listen to her crying because she didn't get the boy she wanted.

I got very drunk the first time when I was fifteen
and it was here behind the roman remains.
I leaned over the glass covering them and smelled the polluted air
of smog and shit from the people's houses and
played the role of the girl.
Nobody ever suspected I wasn't a girl.
I couldn't look at any of the people in the eye
because I thought they thought I was just a fat loser.

I got told for the first time by a boy that he had a crush on me
behind the trees in the park.
They have shapes on them that look like vitiligine
and in front of us a homeless man was selling things he found in
a trash can to people who wouldn't take them
while wearing pants that showed his butt cheeks.

My twenty-two-year old friend blows away smoke and tells me
she's done with his *cazzo di paese*
and wants to move to *Londra*.
I nod approvingly and my travelling anxiety fills up my throat
until I can't breathe and I sip water to make it look like I can.

She says her brother is an English citizen
and that she'll work wherever they want her,
that here - shrug - *siamo in Italia* and that we all
will never find a job.
She worked in a stage for six months
for 300 euros per month
and her contract wasn't renewed,
as it happens for all young people.
The boomers want to pay you
with "notoriety", or "experience"
but those things don't buy pasta or sugo.

I go to work to our little Zara store
and there a twenty-five-year-old coworker
tells me
to kill my dreams
because Italy will butcher them if I don't.

I dream of America
of England
and my hands clench and my stomach closes
and my guts are upside down and I stop breathing.
I don't want to move.
I don't want to go there to starve and work
like my friend who ended up in a place
where she does the thirteen-hour shift.

I work on my own to prove the Italians wrong
and I learn English
to move to America
with my guts in my hands.

But then
it's 2020,
and apparently there's no perfect place in the whole entire world.

IR Belletti

Questions I Have About Of Showing Fealty To A King (According To The

Who invented this practice,
and what was their justification?
Was it a king who, suddenly realising his power,
wanted to see what he could make people do?
If so, what else did he ask for?
Did it start when a king got caught
in a compromising position
and had to create a quick excuse?
Or was there some really keen subject
who just wanted to make the king feel a bit more royal?

If a king did invent it, what did his subjects think?
Was the sexual nature seen as radical?
Did the kings openly derive pleasure,
or did everyone pretend that wasn't happening?

Was it only the men who had to suck the king's nipples?
What about his relatives?
Did children do it?
Were there queens
and did they get the same treatment?
Were female breasts sexualised the way they are now?
If images of the ritual survived, would Tumblr ban them?

How exactly was the ritual choreographed?
Did dozens line up to do it in succession?
How long did they have to suck for
and how vigorously?
Both nipples, or just one?
Did people compete to be the most enthusiastic?
Was refusal an act of treachery
and how were traitors punished?
Did anyone rebel by using excessive force, such as biting?
Was it individualised for each king
according to personal preference?

The Ancient Irish Practice
By Sucking His Nipples
National Museum Of Ireland)

What were the sexual norms of the ancient Celts
and was there any room for deviation?
Did they play with power like we do?
Did anyone role play as kings with their partners,
or was that also treasonous?
Did anyone get off on treason?
What kinks did they have back then?
Did the top/bottom dichotomy exist?
Were these kings the original power bottoms?
Who liked refusal so they could give sterner orders,
and who wanted their pleasure withheld?

Who put a stop to the practice, and why?
Did it die out slowly, like a trend,
or end by royal decree?
How many years did it live for?
How do we know it happened at all?
What records survive? Are they trustworthy?
Is the whole thing one person's power fantasy
projected onto those who can't respond?

Will it be your power fantasy
the next time you get laid?
If you had to suck a world leader's nipples,
which one would you pick?

Allie Kerper

Commitment

[i]

Is it ever more than lust and grab, hunt and peck, creep and keep?
Reasoning past need
We often, frenzied, gripped by passion, acquire
Paintings, albums, movies, books
More plate, furniture, crockery
Than any small community might require
And infatuate, gorge daily until one day
Though we continue to see and use
We find ourselves bereft
Desire atticked or basemented, fumbled away
Submerged in familiarity; only the most stubborn
(Whatever changes, tantalizes, threatens to end) still (loosely) holds our interest
Persists in coercing us to admiration

[ii]

Employing so many shifts to negotiate our lives
Simply to wake and live
We compromise and compromise with
Bodies, beds, and sleep
With food, soaps, clothes, and care
And, of all we suffer or choose, only a handful stays with us
One in a thousand mattering most
Rising above its usefulness
Each day does have such high points
But even these change; and they only as root support
As we rise above such necessity
Into our realms of romance, joy and tragedy
Into be and know

[iii]

To return after many years
To movie, song, or photograph
An instance we once knew well (jukebox, cousin)
Can't, perhaps, exactly place
Or had never before actually seen
But reliably of its time
Is not to wallow
But to, sharp as diamond
Penetrate to a lost heart
To know, as we did not then, what we were
And so what we are
The inverse of nostalgia in the moment
Couples living apart then coming together unlike doves

[iv]

Some 40 years ago I first saw my wife and thought:
This is the face I want to see
Every day for the rest of my life
This is the voice I want to hear
The creamy skin I want to touch
This the smile, these the gestures, scent in sunlight
This precision, agility, beauty, grace
The way she anchors herself in space
This mode of thought, this warm embrace
And it came to pass:
I have had her beside me
Every day, year after year
And every day my thankfulness grows

[v]

All fine, true and sufficient
But it is a truth split, like logs
For the hearth to warm you
It is only fit as well to recall
That when, as a child, I looked
In the mirror of young women's eyes
I learned I was botched, unlovable
Though I could already write a tell
Hit a ball a country mile
Run like the wind
Solve equations, protect the weak
I would properly spend my life alone
Incompetent, unsung

[vi]

So from 8 to 27, in the blindness and desperation of youth
I loved hundreds of women
Would have devoted myself to each
Did to two or three
Happily, most showed no interest and none stuck
Nor would any have served my turn
I was then more susceptible of change
Than at any time since
I was then a traitor to DNA
Willing to risk everything everyday
For the smallest return
Did not believe I had a single skill, a single right
That I was made for joy

[vii]

It can require patience, study, struggle
And it's crucial to recognize, when the time comes, what matters most
The pure trajectory to the condition of fire
What is permanent and what will pass
We must gleam, "wax lovable," flog ourselves, commit without reserve
Surrender everything we had until then sagely valued
Freedom, ambition, longing
For what is in prospect a new freedom
Aware that, it may in time
Decline to disappointment, habit, even prison
Everything depends on preparation/readiness
And that we choose well and keep faith with our choice
Trusting that we can, against all odds, submit/succeed

Alan Cohen

Accidental Prose: 19 Short News Stories (from *An Unfinished Dance*)

*

You wonder what to do with a house full of silence. Sell it. Silence is a highly marketable commodity these days. Think of the all mega-cities, in any one of those cities you could sell houses full of silence for an absolute fortune. It's a bad joke and accidental but in this case silence really is golden.

*

Hail! Toilers at the coalface of miserable existence: consider the frequent floods that blight your lives; the torrents of dead birds that fall from the sky and fierce winds that crush and flatten everything in their path. They are no accident. Look to your vehicles, if you have such, and to decade upon decade of burning fossil fuels. Then curse those who doubted global warming. Especially the bearded phoney ecologist who sought sanctuary in the antipodes after, it's alleged, taking dubious money from oil interests.

*

I told you he was dead grumpy the last time I met him. This was before his stroke. I should've seen it coming because he was very unlike himself but everything is easy with hindsight. He calls it his accident. He's euphemistic, and philosophical, glad to be alive you might say.

*

Martin Eden, accidently on purpose, fell out of a port-hole. It was like he was the Master Ludi from the *Glass Bead Game.* I've never come across two novels with such similar endings. Both books appear to suggest that there is something about drowning that is somehow redemptive. What percentage of suicides has been by drowning? What percentage has been accidental and not suicide at all? If you try to think of all the recorded suicides in the history of humanity, factor in the inevitability of human error, it is only rational to conclude that some of those 'recorded suicides' must be errors. Accidents, no less than just a poor soul who has gone for a swim in some river or sea and been drowned by circumstances outwith their control; the attribution of suicide coming from a certain weight of evidence that those who remain alive were wont to sift. The problem is of course the dead won't tell us. The poet Robert Tannahill of Paisley is a particularly poignant case in this regard. Was his drowning in the night of May 17 1810 an accident? Was it a warm night in May and he was merely trying to cool down? Or was it a deliberate act? The evidence points to suicide but in truth we really can't be sure. There is room for doubt, and there is room to doubt doubt also, a fascinating problem for someone like David Hume to consider. Alas Hume had died in 1776 at which time Tannahill was but two years of age and without a poem or song to his name. And Hume on his death bed perhaps not realising quite the gravity with which history twists us round its grubby little fingers, or perhaps, all too aware of the accidental nature of time.

*

It was only a persona of you. You and not you: a dangerously dark sycophantic ranter; an accidental antichrist.

*

Only the police understand what motivates murderers…

    …them, and somehow by accident, Agatha Christie.

*

You encourage decay. You are walking entropy, a dead energy without the necessary zeal to forestall the chaos you create and attract. You fall into it. You're a living accident. Things plummet and break. Living things die, and somehow it all comes down to the second law of thermodynamics. Apparently "entropy wins when organisms cease to take in energy and die." Shit, eh?

*

Speaking personally... Is there any other way to speak? Maybe ventriloquism but that apart of course I am speaking for myself. What I really mean is, intimately speaking: to communicate with you now on intimate terms I'll share a thought I do not usually express out loud; *how disgusting I find it to have been born in the same country as the poet Robert Burns.* This is in fact only an accident of birth, but let's face it birth is the biggest accident that happens in life. The only people you can blame for this monstrous mishap are your poor unsuspecting parents. The fools, why didn't they take precautions?

Anyway, to return to Robert Burns, (whose dates are 1659 to 1796): so it was in 1659 when the first accident occurred in the life of Burns and sometime in the January of that year he was, indeed, quite accidently, born. I need only hear a few syllables of the man's poetry to be instantly filled with a total hatred for all things Scottish, including myself. Were Burns to have never existed perhaps I would have been spared the torture of such self loathing. What's worse is that my memory now fails me and I can't really remember which came first. Was I really driven to self loathing by the poetry of Robert Burns. Or did I already loath myself and only realise it fully when I heard the poems of Burns in Primary 2. Ah childhood, that's a river I'll never be diving into again.

Another thing about Burns is that he appears to have had an incredible longevity, apparently only dying eventually at the age of one hundred and thirty six or seven. Nice work if you can get it.

*

This is certainly **not** poetry.

Nor is it a saucepan. It's not even a pipe. Even in French, *Ceci n'est pas une pipe.* Mmmmm ... *n'est pas une pipe ... pipe.*

I know you stole that, Rene Magritte, you can't fool me; an accident my arse.

*

Try not to be pre-occupied with other moments, try to live in the moment you're in... You're like a Buddhist when you're at the hairdressers, in the haircutting moment ... in my experience, and yes ... I think your haircut turned out quite well. I'm very bad at the small conversations with the hair-cutting people. If you are too perhaps we should stay at home together and cut each others' hair. You think so? No, too risky. I'd never accidentally cut off your ear. That's crazy. A modern Van Gough, no chance, I can't even paint a wall.

This is not a painting of a wall.

*

How she forgets things these days. She's forgotten herself and other people. Everyone knows the terrifying sadness of it. There but for the grace of god and all that nonsense. It has a pathology like any other illness. It's not an accident of life, it is not inevitable. There are treatments, there will be better treatments. Our understanding remains at a fairly early stage but medical interventions are possible. We are all doomed to die but not to lose ourselves while still rich in life. Let optimism flourish. Let Glasgow flourish; birds, bells, trees and fishes.

*

For excellence in the specific field of creating an internet connection through a large fruit-cake or pudding (what the Scots call a cloughty-dumpling) and showing how the network connection may be enhanced by the use of additional custard she was awarded the Andrew Carnegie Memorial Award. The award reflects the recipient's truly revolutionary contribution to technological advancement in the 21st century.

Later, the addition of the custard was discovered to have been a laboratory accident during the lunch hour. This woman was no Marie Curie and didn't like anything radioactive. Never the less because of the erudition of her paper on the subject the award was allowed to stand.

*

I told the publisher that there was no prospect of my writing a biography of the invisible woman. She hadn't left a trace of her existence anywhere. I told them I couldn't write about a woman who had so totally expunged herself from all and any possible historical narratives. It would be like trying to draw a blank, a character without definition. H. G. Wells managed to write the story of the invisible man back in 1897 but his invisible man had accidently left a trail behind. In reality, or at a subconscious level, Wells's man did not want to be invisible. But this woman, she really knew what she was doing. She was a fantastic success and by dint of her triumph her story must remain untold, at least by me. She was and remains the historical equivalent of what physicists call 'dark matter'.

*

The narrators were accidently omnipotent. However, the entire book was apocryphal. God it makes you wonder if anything's true. Loaves and fishes... an accident... surely not?

*

Even if *The Bucket Rider* was already dead it is clear that Kafka was very familiar with the concept of fuel-poverty. This thoroughly vindicates my view that the arrest of Josef K was no accident. K's arrest was in fact the expression of an ideological terror campaign akin to the deliberate denial of access to food, medicine, water and fuel that a large minority of the world's population experience today. Where was K's access to justice? Where is any one's? How the impoverished freeze in winter: it is heart warming that a cursory study of literature enlightens us so: though art can't stop them from freezing anymore than religion can.

*

I was very gently trying to squeeze the pus from a spot on the forehead of a friend when accidently and without warning the damn thing exploded, filling my eyes with custardy goo. 'God that was sore,' said my friend. 'I'm blind, I'm blind,' I replied.

*

You miserable starvelings who blight the lives of the cheerfully wealthy! Return to your bombed out villages, crumbling dwellings and relatives who are too sick to travel, there's nothing for you here. But should you accidently choose to stay, we can accidently bomb your villages again and again and again.

*

The problem with art is that people, who ever *people* are, expect some kind of shape and form. Whoever *they* are, they expect a beginning, a middle and an end, or a dénouement. Or, something they can interpret as having a certain and definite meaning. Mostly this is a mistake, an accident. Life is not like that, mostly, and neither is art. Music has the greatest freedom but even in music I feel a certain circumscription. Circumscription! Not the easiest word to say. It contains its own meaning. The pronunciation of circumscription is circumscribed. I could go on.

> No.
> I won't.

*

Here comes Jesus. He was accidently betrayed by Judas you know.

*

Jim Ferguson

I Fall In Love With A Plague Doctor

I fall in love with a plague doctor,
with the pockmarked face behind his mask,
the curve of his beak, his leather cloak;

spend quality time with my daughter,
paint rainbows, take her boredom to task
with a song and a dance, to invoke

the spirit of the blitz, the slaughter
of innocents and idiots: ask
who the applause is for, if the smoke

from chimneys, the cross daubed on my door,
are history homework; if a cask
of Spanish sherry, quaffed at the stroke

of midnight, behind walls of Usher,
chanting ring-a-rosey at the masque,
is a gothic fable, or what broke

my fevered crown.

He brings me leeches,
a straight razor and a bowl to catch
my blood; outside, the creak of cart wheels,

the nosegay scent of spice and peaches,
as the tallyman ferries a batch
of souls to the lime pits, as the keels

of cruise ships run aground on beaches
and a bat escapes each cargo hatch,
becomes a wolf and takes to its heels

in a vampire romance, which teaches
us to lock and bar our doors, to latch
our windows, trust isolation heals

when hymns and garlic fail, when breaches
of faith, of government guidelines, match
predicted curves: this is how it feels

to fall in love with a plague doctor.

John Wilks

CONTRIBUTORS

Gale Acuff has had had poetry published in *Ascent, Reed, Poet Lore, Chiron Review, Cardiff Review, Poem, Adirondack Review, Florida Review, Slant, Nebo, Arkansas Review, South Dakota Review, Roanoke Review*, and many other journals in a dozen countries. He has authored three books of poetry: *Buffalo Nickel, The Weight of the World*, and *The Story of My Lives*. He has taught university English courses in the US, China, and Palestine.

Ed Ahern resumed writing after forty odd years in foreign intelligence and international sales. He's had over three hundred stories and poems published so far, and six books. Ed works the other side of writing at *Bewildering Stories*, where he sits on the review board and manages a posse of six review editors.

IR Belletti is a bigender and queer writer from Italy. Sie is an undergraduate currently studying American Literature. Hir previous publications include two poems in 2020, and a short sci-fi story in 2018. When sie doesn't write, sie trains to become as strong as Killuaa Zoldyck and reads sci-fi stories where the lgbt characters survive.

Alan Cohen was a poet before beginning his career as a Primary Care MD, teacher, and manager, and has been living a full and varied life. He has been writing poems for 60 years and is beginning now to share some of his discoveries. He's been married to Anita for 41 years, and they've been in Eugene, OR these past 11.

Milton P. Ehrlich Ph.D. is an 89-year-old psychologist and a veteran of the Korean War. He has published poems in *Poetry Review, The Antigonish Review, London Grip, Arc Poetry Magazine, Descant Literary Magazine, Wisconsin Review, Red Wheelbarrow*, and the *New York Times*.

Jim Ferguson is a Glasgow-based writer. The full version of *An Unfinished Dance* will be published by Rymour Books later in 2021.

Allie Kerper is currently pursuing an MFA in Creative Writing at the University of Glasgow and holds an MSc in Creative Writing from the University of Edinburgh. Her poetry has previously appeared in *Neon, SPAM zine, Adjacent Pineapple*, and elsewhere.

Paweł Markiewicz was born 1983 in Siemiatycze in Poland. He is poet who lives in Bielsk Podlaski and writes tender poems and haiku as well as long poems. Paweł has published his poetries in many magazines. He writes in English and German.

Bruach Mhor likes Organ/Drums/Guitar jazz trios. His poems have appeared in *The Interpreter's House, Ink+Sweat and Tears, Dreich, Broken Spine, The Beach Hut, Re-Side, Morphrog, The Lake* and *Poetry Village.*

Zach Murphy is a Hawaii-born writer with a background in cinema. His stories appear in *Adelaide Literary Magazine, Ghost City Review, Spelk Fiction, Door = Jar, Levitate, Yellow Medicine Review, Ellipsis Zine, Wilderness House Literary Review, Drunk Monkeys*, and *Flash: The International Short-Short Story Magazine.* He lives with his wonderful wife Kelly in St. Paul, Minnesota.

Simon Nagel is a writer from California who now finds himself in the UK. His work has appeared in *Ellipsis Zine, Skyway Journal*, and *Taco Bell Quarterly.* He's finishing a novel.

Nidhi Panandikar is an architect by profession and a portrait photographer by passion. She is a polyglot born in India. Her penchant for creative writing comes from travelling to over 25 countries. Her aim in life is to create a platform for architectural journalism in a political environment.

Yash Seyedbagheri is a graduate of Colorado State University's MFA fiction program. His stories, *"Soon", "How To Be A Good Episcopalian"* and *"Tales From A Communion Line"* have been nominated for Pushcarts. Yash's work has been published in *The Journal of Compressed Creative Arts, Write City Magazine*, and *Ariel Chart*, among others.

Penny Sharman is a published poet, photographer, artist and therapist. She is inspired by wild natural landscapes and the relationships between the seen and the unseen. Penny has an MA in Creative Writing from Edge Hill University. Penny's pamphlet *Fair Ground* (Yaffle Press), her 1st collection *Swim With Me In Deep Water* (Cerasus Poetry) and her 2nd collection *The Day before Joy (*Knives Forks & Spoons Press) are available to buy from her website: pennysharman.co.uk

Shiyang Su is an international student who is currently studying creative writing. She loves writing poems and she is a firm believer of "Show Don't Tell". Her favorite poet is Sharon Olds. Her poems have been published on *Antimatter Dreams* and are forthcoming on *Neologism Poetry Journal, The Bitchin's Kitsch*, and *Dreich Magazine Press.*

John Wilks is the Editor-in-Chief of Cerasus Poetry and Associate Editor of Cerasus Magazine.